Dedicated To:
Marty, my cousin

Written By: Abigail Gartland

I was born in Peru in 1579!

When I was 12, I learned from a doctor and was able to help him treat sick people.

I knew God wanted me to serve people in any way I could.

I helped those who were sick...

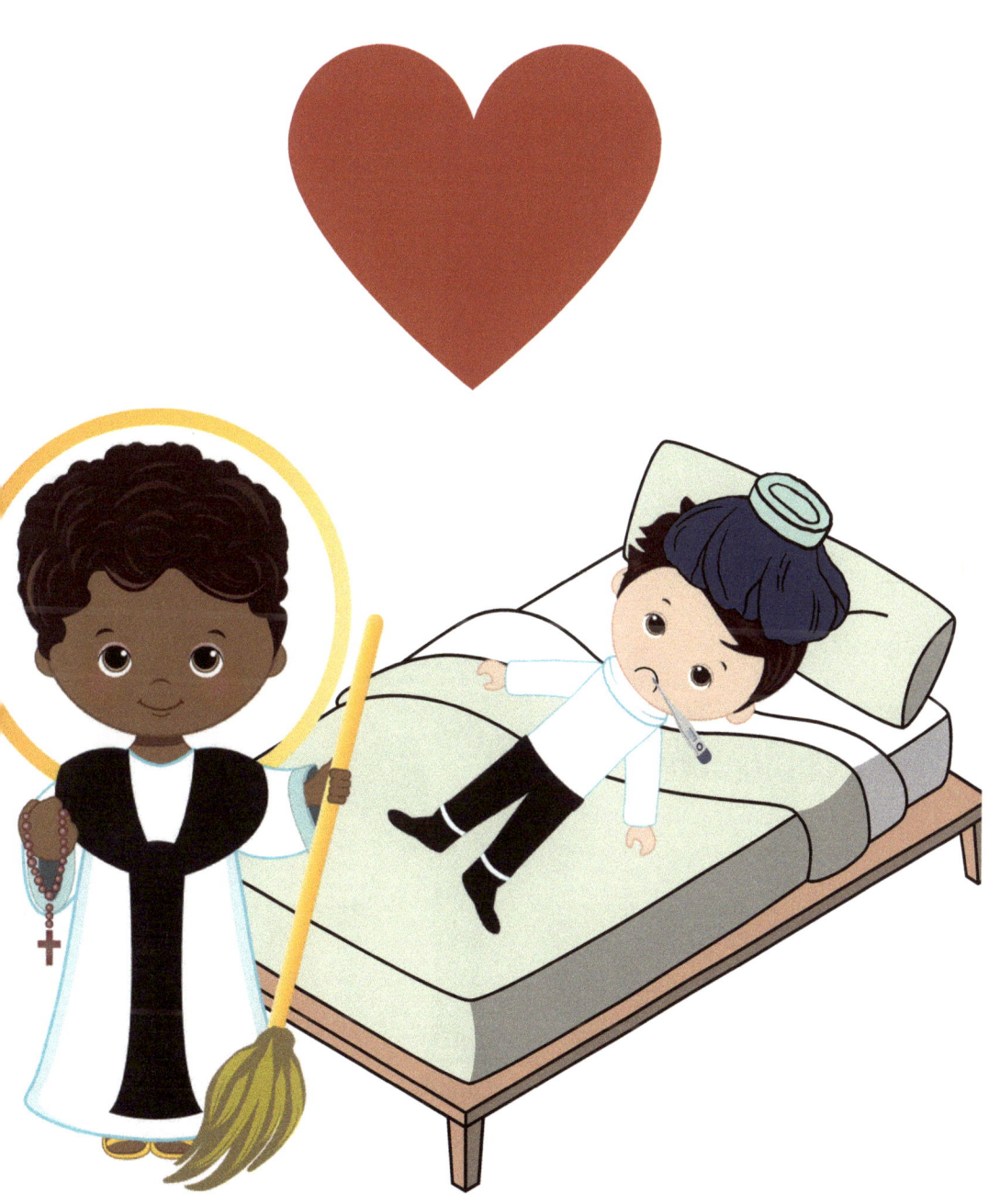

I helped those who were sad...

I helped those who were scared...

I helped those who were angry...

...and I helped those who were lonely.

By helping others, I served Jesus, too. I fell in love with following Jesus' example of serving others.

My favorite thing to do was to spend time with Jesus in Adoration.

Jesus is real and alive in the Eucharist at Mass.

Throughout my life, there were many people who were mean to me.

But I trusted that Jesus would always love and protect me.

Do you want to be more like me?

You can celebrate my feast day with me on November 3rd!

I am the patron saint of social justice!

That means to make sure everything is fair!

I pray for you every day of your life.

St. Martin De Porres, Pray for Us

Copyright:

Clipart: © PentoolPixie © LimeandKiwiDesigns
Licensed purchased: 1/10/2024

About the Author

Abigail Gartland

I love the saints and I love my faith. The idea for sharing the stories of the saints with little ones came when my dear friends were expecting their first baby. I wanted to create something as unique and special as our friendship. Each book is dedicated to very special people and groups who have enriched my faith in different ways. I am blessed to write these stories and appreciate the unending support of my family and friends. When I am not writing, I am a middle school teacher. I hope you enjoy these stories. I pray for each and every person who opens one of my books to learn more about the saints.

Abbie

www.ingramcontent.com/pod-product-compliance
Lightning Source LLC
LaVergne TN
LVHW051043070526
838201LV00067B/4901